NO HANDS ALLOWED
A Robbie Reader

Josh Wolff
Three-Team Player

Marylou Morano Kjelle

Mitchell Lane
PUBLISHERS

P.O. Box 196
Hockessin, Delaware 19707
Visit us on the web: www.mitchelllane.com
Comments? email us: mitchelllane@mitchelllane.com

Copyright © 2006 by Mitchell Lane Publishers. All rights reserved. No part of this book may be reproduced without written permission from the publisher. Printed and bound in the United States of America.

Printing 1 2 3 4 5 6 7 8

**A Robbie Reader
No Hands Allowed**

Brandi Chastain
David Beckham
Landon Donovan

Brian McBride
Freddy Adu

DaMarcus Beasley
Josh Wolff

Library of Congress Cataloging-in-Publication Data
　Kjelle, Marylou Morano.
　　Josh Wolff / by Marylou Morano Kjelle.
　　p. cm. — (Robbie reader. No hands allowed)
　　Includes bibliographical references and index.
　　ISBN 1-58415-388-1 (library bound)
　　1. Wolff, Josh, 1977–Juvenile literature. 2. Soccer players–United States–Biography–Juvenile literature. I. Title II. Series.
GV942.7.W64K44 2006
796.334'092–dc22

2005012781

ABOUT THE AUTHOR: Marylou Morano Kjelle is a freelance writer who lives and works in central New Jersey. She is a regular contributor to several local newspaper and online publications. Marylou writes a column for the Westfield Leader/Times of Scotch Plains-Fanwood called "Children's Book Nook," where she reviews children's books. She has written over twenty nonfiction books for young readers, and she has coauthored and edited others. Other titles she has written for Mitchell Lane are *Alex Rodriguez* and *Tony Hawk*. Marylou has a M.S. degree in Science from Rutgers University and teaches both science and writing at a community college in New Jersey.

PHOTO CREDITS: Cover–Andy Mead/WireImage; pp. 1, 3, 26 (top)–Dave Kaup/Getty Images; p. 4–Tannen Maury/AFP/Getty Images; p. 6 (top)–Tom Pidgeon/Allsport; p. 6 (bottom)–David Maxwell/AFP/Getty Images; p. 8–David Leah/Allsport; p. 10–Harry How/Getty Images; p. 12–Stephen Dunn/Allsport; pp. 15, 22–Jonathan Daniel/MLS/Getty Images; p. 16–Robert Cianflone/Allsport; p. 19–Stephen Dunn/Getty Images; p. 21–Brian Bahr/Allsport; p. 25–Rafael Suanes/WireImage; p. 26 (bottom)–Eric Schlueter/MLSNETImages.

ACKNOWLEDGMENTS: The following story has been thoroughly researched, and to the best of our knowledge and represents a true story. While every possible effort has been made to ensure accuracy, the publisher will not assume liability for damages caused by inaccuracies in the data. This story has been approved for print by Josh Wolff and his agent, Dan Segal.

TABLE OF CONTENTS

Chapter One
A Team Player 5

Chapter Two
Growing Up 9

Chapter Three
Joining Major League Soccer 13

Chapter Four
A Three-Team Player 17

Chapter Five
Year of the Wolff 23

Chronology 27–28
Glossary 28–29
Find Out More 29–31
Index 32

The U.S. Men's National Team played the team from Mexico on February 28, 2001 in Ohio. The game was one of the qualifiers for the 2002 World Cup. Josh's one goal and one assist helped the United States beat Mexico 2-0.

CHAPTER ONE

A Team Player

Every four years, soccer teams from all over the world compete in the World Cup Games. The team that wins this **competition** is considered the best soccer team in the world.

Before a team can play in the World Cup, it must first **qualify**. On February 28, 2001, a qualifying game for the 2002 World Cup was held in Columbus, Ohio. The U.S. Men's National Team was playing against the team from Mexico.

Josh Wolff and his friend Clint Mathis were on the field. It was the start of the second half of the game, and neither team had scored. The ball came to Clint. He sent it to Josh. Josh cut through two members of the Mexican team and kicked the ball toward the Mexican goalie.

CHAPTER ONE

When it comes to playing soccer, Josh can think on his feet and keep his opponent wondering what he will do next. At this game against Mexico, Josh zipped by two Mexican defenders to score the first goal of the game.

Josh is always happy when his team wins. Here he is celebrating the 2-0 win against Mexico on February 28, 2001 in Ohio. Josh once called this his most memorable moment of playing soccer internationally.

A TEAM PLAYER

The goalie stopped the ball and it came back to Josh. With a swift kick, Josh sent the ball into the net.

Josh's goal broke the deadlock with the Mexican team. The score was now 1-0.

Later in the same game, Josh **assisted** another team member, who scored a second goal. The United States beat Mexico 2-0.

"I'm a guy who likes to run down the ball," Josh said.

That same year, Josh scored in another World Cup qualifying game. This time the U.S. was playing against Costa Rica. Josh made the only goal in his team's 1-0 victory over Costa Rica.

The U.S. team made it only as far as the **quarterfinals**, and Brazil won the World Cup in 2002. Although he was disappointed, Josh was glad he had the chance to play for his country.

"Anytime you . . . play for the national team, it's one of the highest marks of your career," Josh said.

Josh has had his share of injuries from playing soccer. Still, he has always returned to the game a stronger and more focused player. The year 2004 was a good one for him, and he was relatively injury-free.

CHAPTER TWO

Growing Up

Josh Wolff was born on February 25, 1977, in Lake Worth, Florida. He was the baby of the family. He had two older brothers. Rick is five years older than Josh, and John is seven years older.

Josh started playing soccer when he was about five years old. His brothers played the game, so he played, too. At first Josh didn't even know what soccer was. "I just . . . ran around and played," he said.

When Josh was ten years old, he and his family moved to Stone Mountain, Georgia. Around the same time, Josh watched his first soccer game on TV. He saw that soccer is more than running around and kicking a ball.

CHAPTER TWO

Josh honors the American Flag before the World Cup game on June 4, 2005 in Salt Lake City, Utah. At this game the U.S. Men's Team played Costa Rica and won 3-0.

GROWING UP

Josh joined the Georgia Youth Soccer Program. He played many different positions, but he liked forward the best. A forward is the player who plays closest to the other team's goal. Sometimes a forward is called a striker. Josh knows the player in this position has a big **impact** on the game.

Soon Josh was playing on the same teams as his older brothers. He had to work hard to play as well as they did. Their mother, Sandy, was their biggest fan. She went to all their games.

Josh grew to be 5 feet 8 inches tall. He weighed 160 pounds. Josh played soccer in Parkview High School. He was captain of the soccer team in his third and fourth years. He was named most valuable player in his last three years. When he was a high school **senior**, Josh was named Georgia State Player of the Year.

Josh attended the University of South Carolina to earn a business degree and play with the school's soccer team, the Gamecocks. In his first and third seasons, the Gamecocks were one of the top five soccer teams in the country. After his junior year in college, Josh was named to the Academic All-American Soccer Team.

CHAPTER THREE

Joining Major League Soccer

After high school, Josh went to the University of South Carolina to study business. He played soccer for the college team, the Gamecocks. In three years of college soccer, Josh scored 21 goals and had eight assists in 43 games. In his first and third seasons, the Gamecocks were one of the top five soccer teams in the country.

While he was in college, Josh joined the Under-20 National Team. All the players on this team were under 20 years old. In 1997, Josh played in the World University Games in Italy and the 1997 Youth Championship Games in Malaysia. The team came in third place. Josh led the U.S. in assists and goals.

CHAPTER THREE

As Josh was learning the game of soccer, he played a lot of different positions. While he attended the University of South Carolina, he played with his college team, the Gamecocks (shown above). Today Josh is considered to be one of the best-playing forwards in soccer history.

JOINING MAJOR LEAGUE SOCCER

In 1998, after his **junior** year in college, Josh was named to the Academic All-American Soccer Team. It is an award that honors players who are good students as well as good athletes.

Josh left college to join the Nike Project 40, a program that **recruits** players for the professional **leagues**. This program gave coaches the chance to see what a good soccer player Josh was. Josh was picked to play with the Chicago Fire. He set the Major League Soccer (MLS) Rookie Record by scoring 8 goals in 14 games.

The first season Josh was with the Chicago Fire, the team won two important competitions —the MLS Cup and the U.S. Open Cup. Josh stayed with the Chicago team for five years. In 2003 he was traded to the Kansas City Wizards. He spent most of the 2003 season recovering from injuries.

One of the highlights of Josh's career has been to represent the United States at the 2000 Olympics in Sydney, Australia. Here Josh plays against a member of the team from Spain on September 23, 2000.

CHAPTER FOUR

A Three-Team Player

Josh plays soccer for three teams. He plays for the Kansas City Wizards. He plays for the U.S. Men's National Team. He has also been on the U.S. Olympic Team. In 2000, Josh started every game for the U.S. at the Olympics in Sydney, Australia. "The Olympics were incredible," he said. He played in all six games and scored two goals. The U.S. team came in fourth place—one place short of a medal. Still, it was better than the team had ever played in the Olympic Games before.

Josh would like to be in the starting lineup of every game. But he knows that he is a good **reserve** as well. "Any minutes [playing] are good minutes," he said.

Josh has his own way of practicing for a game. He **juggles**. He first juggles using his

17

CHAPTER FOUR

thighs, feet, or head. Then he juggles using all parts of his body together. For him, juggling has been a good way to learn how to handle a soccer ball. "When you use your head for juggling, make sure to use your forehead and not the top of your head," he advises.

Josh has been injured many times at games. He has had knee, ankle, and rib injuries. "I do my best to keep fit and stay healthy, but these things just happen," Josh said. His injuries have caused him to miss more games than any other player. At times, the disappointment of getting injured and not being able to play soccer hurt Josh more than the injuries themselves. Each time he has been hurt, Josh has had to work hard to get healthy again. "When I am healthy, I am able to do some good things," Josh said.

Looking forward to playing on the World Cup and Olympic teams has helped him recover. Josh's positive attitude has always returned him to the game stronger than ever.

Josh knows that he must be physically fit to play well. He always warms up before each

A THREE-TEAM PLAYER

Josh performed some fancy moves while juggling and kept the ball away from his opponent in a game against Cuba in January 2002. The United States won this game 1-0.

CHAPTER FOUR

game. He stretches and runs to strengthen his legs. He trains and practices, even in the off-season.

His position as a forward is an important one. Josh is a fast runner with a powerful kick. He is good at thinking on his feet and at guessing what his **opponents** are going to do next. Josh is also good at cutting through their defenses. When he darts around the soccer field, his opponents can't keep track of him. He can dart past many **defenders** on his way to a goal. Even so, he is a good sport. "You have to respect your opponent," said Josh.

Whether playing for an MLS team, the U.S. Men's National Team, or the Olympic Team, Josh is a strong force on the field.

A THREE-TEAM PLAYER

The United States team played against Costa Rica in April 2001. Josh made the only goal in the 1-0 game. Even with Josh's help, the U.S. team only made it as far as the quarterfinals, and Brazil won the World Cup in 2002.

As a member of the Kansas City Wizards, Josh sometimes plays against his old team, the Chicago Fire. Josh was a member of the Chicago Fire from 1998–2003.

CHAPTER FIVE

Year of the Wolff

The year 2004 was good for Josh. He entered the season fit and healthy and started 25 games as a Wizards player. This was more games than in any other season. He spent most of his time on the field playing soccer—a total of 2,252 minutes. He finished the year with the Wizards with 10 goals and 7 assists. He was named to the 2004 Western Conference All-Star Reserve. With Josh's help, the Kansas City Wizards won the 2004 U.S. Open Cup Championship.

Although Josh must spend a lot of time practicing and playing soccer for the U.S. Men's National Team and the Kansas City Wizards, he still spends with his family. In 2000, Josh married Angela Kelley. They have

CHAPTER FIVE

two sons. Tyler David was born in February 2003, and Owen was born in December 2004.

Josh likes to ride his bike and to play golf with his friends on the weekends. He also likes eating out. His favorite foods are Italian and Mexican.

Josh has helped the U.S. National Soccer Team Players Association raise money to fight the blood cancers leukemia and lymphoma. He taped an announcement that was read over the public address systems of schools throughout the country. Josh asked students to give spare change to help in the fight against these two diseases.

Josh has goals for the future. He wants to finish earning his college degree. He would also like to someday play in Europe with European soccer teams. But for now, Josh has his eye on the 2006 World Cup Games, which will be held in Germany.

"It's going to be a heck of a game," he said.

A STAR AT HOME

Josh tries to keep control of the ball in this 2006 World Cup Qualifier Game against Panama on October 13, 2004. The United States won this game 6-0.

CHAPTER FIVE

The 2005 Kansas City Wizards. Players standing in back row from left to right: Jimmy Conrad, Jack Jewsbury, Sasha Victorine, Chris Klein, Jose Burciaga Jr., and goalie Bo Oshoniyi; front row from left to right: Diego Gutierrez, Nick Garcia, Davy Arnaud, Josh Wolff, and Kerry Zavagnin.

Josh tries to cut through two players from the Des Moines Menace at a game at Julien Field on August 3, 2005. The Wizards won 6-1.

26

CHRONOLOGY

1977   Josh Wolff is born on February 25.

1995   He is named Georgia State Player of the Year.

1997   He plays in the World University Games in Italy and the Youth Championship Games in Malaysia.

1998   He is named to Academic All-American Soccer Team. He enters Major League Soccer when he is assigned to the Chicago Fire. He receives the first ever Chevrolet Young Male Athlete of the Year Award. He sets the MLS Rookie Record by scoring 8 goals in 14 games.

2000   He plays for the U.S. at the Olympics in Sydney. He marries Angela.

2001   He wins Chevrolet Man of the Match for February 28 game against Mexico.

2002   He helps the U.S. National Team win a Gold Cup.

2003   He is traded to the Kansas City Wizards.

2004   He is named to the 2004 Western Conference All-Star Reserve. He helps the Wizards win the U.S. Open Cup.

CHRONOLOGY

2005 He practices and prepares for the 2006 World Cup Games while he continues to play for the Kansas City Wizards.

GLOSSARY

assist (uh-SYST)—to pass the ball to a team member who can shoot on goal.

competition (com-peh-TIH-shun)—a contest.

defender (de-FEN-der)—the player who protects the goal area in soccer.

impact (IM-pact)—a major effect or difference.

juggle (JUG-gul)—to keep a ball or balls in the air without letting them hit the ground. A soccer ball is juggled with any part of the body except hands and arms.

junior (JEW-nyer)—a student in the third year of high school or college.

league (leeg)—a group of matched teams that compete against one another.

opponent (uh-POE-nent)—the team or team member against whom you are playing.

GLOSSARY

qualify (KWAH-lih-fye)—to win games to prove you are ready to play in tougher competitions.

quarterfinals (KWAR-ter-FYE-nals)—the part of a tournament that determines who will stay to play in the next round.

recruit (ree-KROOT)—to look for and attract a new member.

reserve (ree-ZERV)—a player that is not put on the field at the beginning of the game.

senior (SEEN-yor)— the last (fourth) year of high school or college.

FIND OUT MORE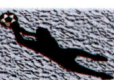

Book
Crisfield, Deborah. *The Everything Kids' Soccer Book: Rules, Techniques, and More About Your Favorite Sport!* Avon, Mass.: Adams Media, 2002.

Web Addresses
ESPN Soccernet
http://soccernet.espn.go.com
Major League Soccer
www.mlsnet.com

FIND OUT MORE

Sports Illustrated
http://sportsillustrated.cnn.com/
The United States National Soccer Players
www.ussoccerplayers.com

Works Consulted

Fisher, William. "For Club or Country." *American Soccer News,* June 8, 2004, www.cybersoccernews.com/mls/mlsnews/040508club_v_country.shtml (April 1, 2005).

Halperin, Andy. "Q & A: Soccer's Josh Wolff on the Olympics and Head-tennis." U.S. Olympic Team, April 22, 2002, http://www.usoc.org/27555_12284.htm (March 24, 2005).

"Howling Wolff." *Sports Illustrated,* March 12, 2001, p. 70.

Monfried, Andrew. "Six Good Questions for Josh Wolff." United States National Soccer Players Association, April 26, 2004, http://www.ussoccerplayers.com/game_time/424078.html (January 5, 2005).

FIND OUT MORE

Rosa, Brian. "Josh Wolff." *Round Not Oval: The U.S. Soccer Players Monthly,* October 2004, http://www.ussoccerplayers.com/rno/bonus102004.html (July 26, 2005).

Segal, Dan. Conversations with Josh's agent, August 2005.

"U.S. Forward Josh Wolff Ready to Deliver." Rediff Sports, May 18, 2002, www.rediff.com/sports/2002/may/18wc2.htm (April 1, 2005).

Vecsey, George. "Georgia on Their Minds, the World at Their Feet," *The New York Times,* March 28, 2001, p. D4.

Wolff, Josh. "Juggling with Josh Wolff." n.d., http://www.ussoccerplayers.com/resource_center/resource_center_topics/skills/331342.html (July 26, 2005).

INDEX

Academic All-American Soccer Team 15
Brazil 7
Chicago Fire 15, 22
Columbus, Ohio 5
Costa Rica 7
Gamecocks 12, 13
Georgia State Player of the Year 11
Georgia Youth Soccer 11
Kansas City Wizards 15, 17, 22, 23, 26
Lake Worth, Florida 9
Major League Soccer (MLS) 15, 20
Major League Soccer Team 20
Mathis, Clint 5
Mexican Soccer Team 5, 7
MLS Cup 15
Nike Project 40 15
Parkview High School 11
Stone Mountain, Georgia 9
Sydney, Australia 17
U.S. Men's National Team 4, 5, 17, 19, 20, 23
U.S. National Soccer Team Players Association 24
U.S. Olympic Team 16, 17, 18, 20
U.S. Open Cup 15, 18, 23
Under-20 National Team 13
University of South Carolina 12, 13
Western Conference All-Star Reserve (2004) 23
Wolff, Angela Kelley (wife) 23
Wolff, John (brother) 9, 11, 14
Wolff, Josh
  Born 9
  Injuries 18
  Playing against Mexico 5
  Physical fitness 19
  Position as a forward 19
Wolff, Owen (son) 24
Wolff, Ricky (brother) 9, 11, 14
Wolff, Sandy (mother) 11
Wolff, Tyler David (son) 24
World Cup Games (2002) 5, 6, 7, 21
World Cup Games (2006) 24, 25
World University Games (1997) 13
Youth Championship Games (1997) 13

I Am Your Kitten

This is my book. It tells you how to take care of me when you bring me home to be your new friend. You will find extra facts about me in these bubbles throughout the book.

I Am Your Kitten

By Gill Page

WATERBIRD BOOKS

The Author

Gill Page has been involved with a wide variety of animals for many years. She has run a successful pet center and she has rescued and found new homes for numerous unwanted animals. She has cared for many animals of her own and she would like to pass on her knowledge of animals to children so that they may learn how to care for their pets lovingly and responsibly.

McGraw Hill Children's Publishing

This edition published in the
United States of America in 2004 by
Waterbird Books
an imprint of McGraw-Hill Children's Publishing,
a Division of The McGraw-Hill Companies
8787 Orion Place
Columbus, Ohio 43240-4027

www.MHkids.com

Library of Congress Cataloging-in-Publication Data is on file with the publisher.

© 2000 Interpet Publishing Ltd.
All rights reserved.

All rights reserved. Except as permitted under the United States Copyright Act, no part of this publication may reproduced or distributed in any form or by any means, or stored in a database retrieval system, without prior written permission from the publisher.

Printed in Hong Kong.

ISBN 0-7696-3390-0

1 2 3 4 5 6 7 8 9 10 IPP 09 08 07 06 05 04 03

Credits

Editor: Philip de Ste. Croix
Designer: Phil Clucas MSIAD
U.S. Editors: Joanna Callihan and Catherine Stewart
Production Editor: Lowell Gilbert
Studio photography: Neil Sutherland
Colour artwork: Rod Ferring
Production management: Consortium, Poslingford, Suffolk CO10 8RA

Contents

Making Friends	6
Getting To Know Me	8
Taking Me Home	10
My First Day at Home	12
Toilet Training	14
Time for Bed	16
My Favorite Foods	18
Meal Times	20
Treats and Tidbits	22
Playtime	24
Safe Play	26
Looking My Best	28
My Own Front Door	30
Keeping Fit and Healthy	32
Health Check	34
Girl or Boy?	36
What If I Do Have Kittens?	38
How to Write a Report on Your Pet	40
Kitten Checklist	41
My Relatives	42
A Note to Parents	46
Acknowledgements	48

Making Friends

Hello. I am your new friend. What is your name? I will need a name, too. I am very smart, so I will soon learn to come when you call me. I will tell you a few things about myself in this book, so that you will know how to take care of me. I love playing with toys, and we can play together. You can even make some toys for me. I would like to play with a long piece of string. Since I am young, I will get tired easily. When I am looking sleepy will you put me into my bed so that I can take a nap? Do you have a soft bed? I would like one, too.

When we are friends, we can play all sorts of games together. Don't let me get too tired.

Cats have been living with people for more than 4,000 years.

My mother has shown me how to keep my fur clean by licking it, but you can help by gently brushing me. I like when you pet me, and I will show you how happy I am by purring. I will become very hungry when I am playing. When you have your meals, can you make sure I have mine, too? I will always need a bowl of fresh water to drink when I am thirsty.

Kittens clean their fur by licking it.

Getting To Know Me

Cats come in lots of colors. Cats with tawny, brown, or gray fur and darker streaks or spots are called *tabby* cats. *Tortoise-shell* cats have fur that is black, red, and cream, and they are nearly always girls. *Calico* cats have patches of black, white, red, and cream. Black cats may have white paws. Boy cats are called *toms*, and girl cats are called *queens*. Some of us have long, fluffy hair, but kittens with short hair are easier to care for.

It will be hard to tell what I will look like when I grow up. I may be a big, fat cat, or I could be a small, sleek cat. Some kittens grow very tall, but most will only grow to be about 12 inches (30 cm.) high. When you pick me up, I need to feel safe, and I need to know that you will not drop me. Gently hold me with one hand under my front feet and the other under my back feet and my bottom.

Taking Me Home

You can find a cat in a pet shop, from a family home, or from a rescue center which is a place where stray cats and their kittens are often taken care of. I should be playful and have bright, shiny eyes. If I am sitting very quietly in a corner and I do not want to play, it may be because I am sick. Ask how old I am. I should be eight weeks old before I am taken to my new home. If I am going to be left on my own often, I would like to take a brother or sister with me; then, we will have each other to play with while you are away.

When I was born, I was tiny. I weighed only about 3 ounces (90 grams). That's about the same as a small bar of chocolate!

You will need a pet carrier in order to take me home. I like to see where I am going, so I would really like a carrier with a wire front. To make the carrier cozy, put a blanket in the bottom. If we are going home in a car, put me in a safe place where the carrier can't fall over. If we will be driving for a long time, I would like some water to drink on the way. Most kittens are of mixed breed, like me. There are also purebred cats.

My First Day At Home

I am happy that I will be living with you, but I will probably be frightened on my first day in your house. I may try to hide. If you have a chimney, be sure to ask your mom or dad to put something in front of it so I don't try to climb up it. Keep me in one room that is safe and has no places for me to get stuck. Do you have any other pet friends living with you? If you do, please stay with me when I first meet them. Dogs might chase me, and other cats may hiss at me or scratch me. Soon, we will all be friends, but until we are, leave me in a room on my own when you are out or have gone to bed.

> I may try to scratch or chew things in your house.

I am very nosy and can get into all sorts of trouble. I enjoy climbing up the curtains; although I do look silly when I cannot get back down. That is when you will have to help me. Be sure to put your toys away or I may take them to play with. With lots of love from you,
I know I will be fine.

Toilet Training

Kittens need to learn how to use a litter box. While I am young, I will have to be kept indoors, so I will need something to use as a bathroom. A litter box is a box that does not leak. There are a lot of nice plastic litter boxes to choose from that are easy for you to keep clean. You will have to fill it with cat litter for me to sit in.

When I am properly house-trained, I can be left to play happily indoor for hours.

As soon as you bring me home, put me in my litter box so that I know where it is. If you do this every time I have something to eat or drink, or when I wake up, I will soon learn what it is for. You can even buy me a litter box that has a hood or cover on it. Then, I cannot make a mess by digging in the litter and scattering it all over the floor. The box should be cleaned out every day.

Time For Bed

I like to spend a lot of my time asleep. Is your bed soft and warm? I will want a bed like that too, or I might try and share your bed. I want my bed to be where I can be left alone to rest and where people will not accidentally step on me. There are some really nice beds that you can buy from the pet shop, but I will be just as happy with a large cardboard box.

To keep me safe when I first come to live with you, put my bed into a large, wire cage. Put my litter box in with me and some water for me to drink. Then, I will have all that I need. After I get used to living with you, I will not need to be shut in at night or when you are away. Put a blanket in the bottom of my bed. You have blankets that cover you to keep you warm, but I just sit on mine. Please do not tuck me in or cover me up. It will be hard for me to get out and it could even stop me from breathing.

In cold weather, I may cover my face with my tail to keep it warm.

My Favorite Foods

When I am little, I will need four small meals every day, but by the time I am one year old, I will need only two. You can find out how much food to give me on page 21. Before you bring me home, find out what I have been eating. If you give me the same sort of food to start with, I will not have an upset stomach. After a while, you can try feeding me all kinds of cat food to see which I like the best. If I have a lot of different kinds of food to try when I am young, I will not be fussy about what I eat when I grow up.

When I am a kitten, you should feed me special kitten food until I am at least six months old. I must have a bowl of fresh water too. If I eat or drink too much human food or beverages, I will have a bad stomach ache, so please do not feed me any of your leftovers. I don't like food that is very cold.

Milk is nice, but too much will give me a stomach ache.

Meal Times

I will need two dishes—one for my food and another for my water. You could buy dishes that have my name painted on them. I will know that they are mine, but it won't stop me from taking food from other pet dishes. So that I don't get into trouble, you should stand and watch me when I am eating and stop me from taking food from my friends.

Dishes that are heavy and cannot be pushed around the floor are best. People may get upset if I tip my dish and spill the food. I like my dishes to be kept very clean, so please wash them every day. You will see when I don't like the smell of something because I will walk away and shake my paws at you. We should not share plates, even though I often think the food on your plate is nicer than my own.

Feeding Timetable

I have a small stomach and need only small meals.

- **8–12 weeks old:** Four meals of kitten food a day—breakfast, lunch, afternoon snack, dinner. Three teaspoonfuls at each meal.
- **12–18 weeks:** Three meals a day—breakfast, lunch, dinner. Six to eight teaspoonfuls at each meal.
- **18–26 weeks:** Three meals a day as before, but nine to 12 teaspoonfuls at each meal.
- **26 weeks and older:** Two meals a day—breakfast and supper.

If I am having canned cat food, read and follow the instructions on the can.

Treats and Tidbits

Just like you, I like a few snacks between meals. I must not eat your snacks, though. Salt and chocolate are very bad for me, and they will make me feel ill. The pet shop has some tasty biscuits that have a fishy taste. I love those. If you have a cat door, you can use a treat to show me the way through. Then, I'll know how to go in and out of your house.

I love a bowl like this that has fresh grass in it for me to eat.

A treat I really enjoy is grass. I need to eat the grass to help me digest food, just as you need to eat green vegetables. It adds fiber to my diet and has vitamins. You can buy a little pot from the pet shop that has grass seed in it. When you get home, pour water on it and in a few days grass will grow. It is called *kitty grass* or *cat grass*. Or your parents could dig up a piece of lawn and put in a small pot. Only use clean grass. I will need fresh grass every week.

Playtime

I enjoy playing with my toys as much as you do. Playing with toys when I am young helps to make me fit and strong. Even when I am grown up, I will still want to play games with you. I love to scratch with my claws. If you buy me a scratching post, I will soon learn to sharpen my claws on that and not on the sofa. Parents get very, very upset when I do that.

Some toys have the leaves of a plant called *catnip* in them. I think it has a lovely smell and I will play for hours with a catnip toy. But I am just as happy to play with toys that you have made for me. A cotton reel tied to a long piece of string is a fun toy. I can even have a good time playing hide and seek in a cardboard box or under a page of a newspaper.

When I rub against you, I am leaving my scent mark on you.

Safe Play

Please make sure my play area is safe for me. There are a lot of things in the house that I will like to chew. Electric wires will kill me if I try to eat them. Even if an iron is not plugged in, I could still pull it down on top of me. That will really hurt, so please put away anything that I could hurt myself with. Some of the pretty plants that you have in the house could make me sick if I eat them. Make sure that your plants are out of my reach.

If my whiskers fit through a gap, then I know that the rest of my body will, too.

Ask your parents to look inside the washing machine or dryer before they turn them on. I may be hiding there! As I get bigger, I can play in the yard. I will try and climb trees, but sometimes I cannot find my way down again. You must not try to help me, or we will both be stuck up the tree. Ask a grown-up to help me get down. If you have a cat door, I will need to learn how to use it. That way, I can dash into the house if something frightens me (see pages 30-31).

Looking My Best

I will need some help to keep my fur healthy. I can do most of the grooming myself, but there are some places I cannot reach. My tongue gets very tired, too. You will have to brush me to keep my hair free of tangles. If I have long hair, you will need to brush it every day as well. Wire combs will get the knots out of my fur. Don't tug too hard, though. Bristle brushes make my fur shiny. If I have short hair I will only need to be groomed two or three times a week. Brushing me very gently and a little at a time will show me how nice it is.

My tongue is covered with very fine spikes. I use it like a comb on my fur.

When I am little, I can sit on your lap when you brush me. If I am too big for your lap, stand me on a table that has a towel spread over it to keep me from slipping. Start with my back and always brush my hair from my head toward my tail. I shed my coat twice a year. This is called molting. I feel quite itchy at these times. Combing helps, and it stops my loose fur from sticking to the furniture and to your clothes.

My Own Front Door

If you have a cat door, then I can get in and out when I need to. I will have to be shown how to use one. Before I can go out on my own I will have to get used to wearing a collar. Put a tag on the collar with my name and address on it, in case I get lost. I will not like it it when you first put it on me. Buy me a stretchy one, so that I can wriggle out of it if I get it stuck on a twig or wire. A collar that glows in the dark makes it easy for car drivers to see me at night.

Unlike a dog, when I wag my tail it may mean I am angry.

Show me how the cat door works. Open it and call me through. Offering me one of my favorite treats will make me brave enough to jump through. I will soon learn. I will have to slip through quickly so that my tail will not get shut in the door. If other cats try to come in, you can buy a special cat door and collar that is magnetic. When I am wearing the special collar that unlocks the door, I will be the only cat that can go in and out.

Keeping Fit and Healthy

My doctor is called a *veterinarian*, or *vet*. He will take care of me when I am sick, but he also helps to keep me fit and healthy. When my mother was feeding me with her milk, I was safe from any diseases. Now that I am living with you, I need injections to protect me from cat flu and other nasty sicknesses. The vet will give me my first injections when I am eight or nine weeks old. I will need another one when I am 12 weeks old. I must go back to the vet every year for booster shots.

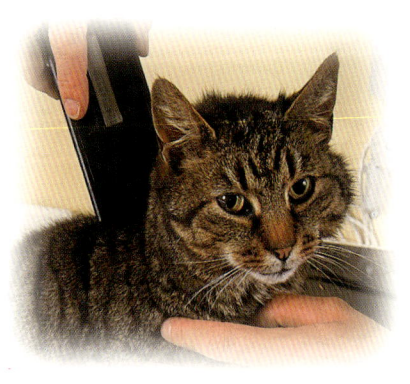

If a microchip is put under my skin, it will be easy for a vet to find out to whom I belong. He can read the chip with a scanner, like this.

I am a kitten now, but I can live to be 17 years old, or even older.

The vet will check me over for other things, too. All cats can have worms. They are special worms that live in my stomach and are very bad for me. The vet has pills that you can give me to kill the worms. He will also check my fur for fleas. The vet can microchip me, so that if I am lost or stolen, my owner can be located. Take me to the vet in a cat carrier. I will not be able to run away, and other animals in the waiting room will not be able to scare me.

Health Check

Here's a list of things to check to make sure I'm healthy and feeling good!

1. Appetite. Am I eating well? Am I getting sick? Do I eat a lot but stay very thin? That may mean I need worm medicine.

2. Breathing. I should breathe easily and quietly, without coughing or choking.

3. Body. I should be lean, but not too skinny. Do I have a clean bottom?

4. Claws. My claws should not be too long or split. I should not have any thorns or splinters in my feet.

5. Coat. My fur should be clean and shiny, without too many loose hairs. I should not have bald patches.

6. Behavior. Am I playful and lively? Alert and attentive? I should not be droopy or tired.

7. Ears. Are they clean so that I can hear everything? They should not be itchy or smelly.

8. Eyes. They should be clear and bright, not sticky or watering, as if I am crying.

9. Mouth and teeth. I should have nice clean teeth and pink gums. I should not have bad breath.

My ears may get ~~dirt~~y inside. Get a grown-~~up~~ to show you how to clean them gently.

If I do not look well or have hurt myself, I need to be taken to the vet quickly. Keep a checklist handy that you can take with you. It should have on it:

- My vet's name
- My vet's telephone number
- My vet's address
- Phone number to the nearest emergency animal hospital
- Address of the nearest emergency animal hospital
- Date of my first injection
- Date of my second injection
- Dates for my booster injections

Girl or Boy?

It is up to you to decide if you would like to have a girl or a boy kitten. There are hundreds of cute kittens like me that want a friend like you to live with. A lot of them are not as lucky as I am and never have a happy home. You will keep me safe and feed and care for me. I do not need to have kittens myself when I grow up. You can take me to the vet for a simple surgery so that I will not become a mom or a dad. If I am a girl cat, I will be spayed. If I am a boy cat, I will be neutered. I will be a bit sleepy when I get home, but after a good rest I will be fine.

I have just had my operation. There is only a little bit of my fur missing. My vet says that the hair will soon grow back.

A girl kitten
♀

A boy kitten
♂

To tell what sex I am, you will have to look under my tail. Girl kittens have two holes close together. Boy kittens also have two holes, but they are further apart. Boy cats that do not have the operation will be rather smelly and will do a lot of fighting. Girl cats will continue to have kittens; this is unhealthy for them, and it is hard to find homes for all the kittens. If you are not sure, the vet will be able to tell you if I am a girl or boy.

To weigh me, first weigh yourself on the bathroom scale, then do it again holding me. Take away your weight from this figure to find mine.

What If I Do Have Kittens?

Just in case I do have kittens, I will show you what to do. I will need a quiet place to care for my babies. I hope you will not touch them too much at first. Give me a large box where the kittens will be safe, but make sure I can still get in and out. I will need extra food so that I can make a lot of milk to feed the kittens.

> My mom carried me in tummy for 65 before I was b

Young kittens need their sleep. Please do not wake us up to play with you.

I can have from one to eight babies. They are born with their eyes closed and their ears folded back. They will not be able to see or hear for a while. I will keep them warm, dry, clean, and safe. At three weeks old, their eyes will be open, their ears will straighten, and they will start to play.

Now, the kittens will need to be fed with a little bit of meat and some milk. Use milk specially made for kittens. When they are eight weeks old, I will not be feeding them any more. They should have four meals a day (see pages 20-21) and will be ready to go to new homes.

How to Write a Report on Your Pet

You may choose to write a report about your pet for school. Start by making an outline of what you would like to say about your pet. The outline should begin with an introduction and end with a conclusion. In between the introduction and the conclusion, you should list three or four characteristics about your pet that you would like to write about.

In the introduction, state your topic, which is your pet, and you should tell the reader what you will be discussing in the rest of your report.

After the introduction, provide the reader with a more detailed description of your pet's characteristics. For instance, you may want to talk about your pet's appearance, your pet's favorite toys, and your pet's quirky mannerisms. Cover these topics in separate paragraphs in your report.

After you finish the detailed description of your pet's characteristics, you should give a short summary of your whole report. Then, you may want to end your report with a funny story about your pet. When you are finished, you will have a wonderful record of your pet that you can return to in years to come.

Kitten Checklist

Daily
1. Wash my plates and water bowls.
2. Feed me and give me fresh water.
3. Brush me.
4. Check my litter box, clean it, and add extra litter.
5. Check me for any cuts and scratches.

Weekly
1. Wash my bedding.
2. Wash out my litter box, dry, and refill it.
3. Health check. Look at the health check list on page 34.
4. Look at my toys. Throw away any that are falling apart. I might choke on or swallow, small, broken pieces.
5. Wash my brush and comb.

My Relatives

The usual kind of cat that you will probably choose as your friend is a crossbreed, like me. I can be one color or a mixture of colors. I may not even be the same color as my brothers or sisters. No matter what color I am, I can be trained to be a great pet!

A bib

A kitten's sock

If a cat is all black, it will look like a little panther. A cat may be called a *blue cat*. It is not really blue, but it has only gray hairs in its coat. A cat may have all-white fur. Choose this cat only if it has brown or green eyes. Cats that are only white and have blue eyes are deaf, usually. Cats will have either short or long hair. They can have white paws, which are called *socks*. If a cat has a white patch under its chin, it is called a *bib*.

My Relatives

You may want to buy a purebred kitten. You will know what I will look like when I am grown up because I will be the same as my mom and dad. Each purebred cat has its own name and its own characteristics that make it easy to recognize.

There are lots of different breeds. A Persian has a lot of long, fluffy hair in a lot of different colors. They have round faces and squashed-up noses. Siamese have short, creamy-colored hair. Their ears, legs, and tails are usually dark brown or blue, but there are other colors, too.

I am a Persian kitten with white fluffy fur.

We are Bengal kittens with "leopard" spots.

A Siamese cat is slim with long, thin legs. Burmese are like Siamese, but they are a little fatter, and their fur is a single color. The Maine Coon is a really large cat. It can be bigger than a small dog. A strange breed is the Rex cat. It has almost no hair at all. Another strange cat is the Turkish Van. These cats love to go swimming. They are white with patches of ginger or cream.

My friends the Manx cats are special. They are born without tails.

~ 45 ~

A Note To Parents

The relationship between child and pet can be a special one. We hope this book will encourage young pet owners to care for their pets responsibly. Studies show that developing positive relationships with pets can contribute to a child's self-esteem and self-confidence.

It is essential to stress that parents also play a crucial role in pet care. Parents need to help children develop responsible behaviors and attitudes toward pets. Children may need supervision while handling pets and caring for them. Parents may need to remind their children that animals—like people—need to be treated with love and respect.

In addition to a happy and suitable home, all pets need food, water, and exercise. Being a pet owner can be a costly and time-consuming experience. Before choosing a pet, be certain that your family's lifestyle is conducive to the type of pet you wish to own. Talk to a local veterinarian if you have questions.

Owning a pet can provide a wonderful opportunity for children to learn about responsibility, compassion, and friendship. We wish your child many years of happiness and fulfillment with his or her new pet!

Acknowledgements

The author and publisher would like to thank the owners who generously allowed their pets to be photographed for this book and the children who agreed to be models. Specifically, they would like to thank Donna and Trevor Strowger and Ellie, Sean and Sam Reeves and Buffy, and Florence Elphick. Thanks also to Stephen Edgington of Hassocks Pet Center, Denis Blades of Gattleys, Storrington, Steyning Pet Shop, Neil Martin of Washington Garden Centre, Washington, Interpet Limited and Farthings Veterinary Group, Billingshurst.

Thanks are due to the following photographers and picture libraries who kindly supplied photographs that are reproduced in this book.
Geoff du Feu/RSPCA Photolibrary: 26, 42.
Angela Hampton/RSPCA Photolibrary: 2, 13, 32, 38, 39, 44, 46.
Marc Henrie: 45.
E.A. Janes/RSPCA Photolibrary: 27.
Alan Robinson/RSPCA Photolibrary: 43.